THE BATSFORD COLOUR BOOK OF THE HIGHLANDS

THE BATSFORD COLOUR BOOK OF
The Highlands

Text and photographs by
Tom Weir

B. T. BATSFORD LTD
LONDON AND SYDNEY

First published 1975

© Tom Weir 1975

Filmset by Servis Filmsetting Ltd, Manchester
Printed and bound by Dai Nippon Printing Co Ltd, Hong Kong
for the publishers B. T. Batsford Ltd, 4 Fitzhardinge Street, London W1
and 23 Cross Street, Brookvale, NSW 2100, Australia

ISBN 0 7134 3004 4

Contents

Introduction

No entry to the Scottish Highlands is more thrilling than the route of the A82 from Glasgow by Loch Lomond, when suddenly the Lowlands are left behind at Balloch and at Duck Bay you look over the broad loch to the mountains rising above a scatter of wooded islands. No need to be told that this is the Highland Boundary Fault, and that the line of demarcation between the low country and the high country is the immediate foreground of islands.

North from here gives perhaps the most varied drive of any loch in Scotland, but the driver must keep his mind on the road for its tight bends and narrowness require absolute concentration. Even so, there are plenty of lay-bys, as beyond Luss (page 17) you begin the zig-zags of the shore lines, with new vistas round every bend, and invitations to stop at Inverbeg and Inveruglas, where you can side-track into Glen Douglas or to Loch Sloy by car to savour the hills.

The essential feature of the view is Ben Lomond, and the rugged east shore, fringed by oak and birch, hung with waterfalls, and with no more than the odd white speck to break the feeling of wilderness. The mighty Ben, first seen as a broad-shouldered spade of summit, becomes a soaring point as you go north, until at last you are looking on the verticalities of its most secret face.

It was by Loch Lomond, that early travellers like William Wordsworth and Sir Walter Scott, reached the Trossachs. Sailing to Inversnaid, they took horse and trap and drove over the hills to Loch Katrine, to be rowed down by sturdy Highlanders to the pass of the Trossachs of which Scott wrote:

> *High on the south Ben Venue*
> *Down on the lake in masses threw,*
> *Crags, knolls, and mounds, confusedly hurled,*
> *The fragments of an earlier world . . .*

Earlier travellers to the Highlands had found little to rhapsodise over amongst the wild glens and Bens of the rugged Highlands, not even the perceptive Thomas Pennant whose classic *Tour in Scotland* launched the sage of Fleet Street, Sam Johnson to put on his cloak, pick up his staff, and set off with his mouthpiece Boswell in 1773 at the age of 64 to tackle the adventurous journey so well described in his *Journey to the Hebrides*. From it we deduce that little as he liked the wild country, he grew to value its people for their human qualities and natural courtesy.

Walter Scott was only two years old when Johnson was enjoying himself so mightily in Skye, even if he was describing it as '. . . a uniformity of barrenness'. Johnson was able to rationalise things by giving reasons for his travels, which were '. . . to become possessed of more certainties, and consequently gain more principles of reasoning, and found a wider base of analogy' (edition 1775, p. 60).

But Sir Walter Scott, by the time he had written his *Lady of the Lake* in 1810 was preaching to a public willing to be converted. Scott prompted the first tourist rush in history to a Highlands symbolised by Loch Lomond and the Trossachs and the tales of Rob Roy. Romance in the wild beauty of the Highlands was easy to find now because of greater ease of travel, as Thomas Telford built his network of roads and bridges, and comfortable hotels and shooting lodges followed.

The Trossachs with its nine lochs and tight-knit little peaks (page 39) is the perfect foil to the great sweep of Loch Lomond with its higher peaks and deeper glens. The river drainage from the Trossachs is into the Forth, whereas Loch Lomond is to the Clyde. Northward of the Trossachs the peaks drain into the Tay on the main watershed of Scotland whose source is Ben Lui (page 21).

From Tyndrum the A82 climbs away from the Tay, northward to Rannoch Moor and Glen Coe. The infant river flows eastward, along Strath Fillan and through Glen Dochart to Killin where it enters Loch Tay. Not until it emerges does it take on the name of River Tay, and one of its first tributaries is the Lyon.

The true entrance to Glen Lyon is at Fortingal where the river tumbles out of a narrow gorge between tree-clad jaws, a place of rioting colour in spring and autumn, when beech, ash, oak, sycamore, birch and larch vie with each other in brilliance. Bridge of Balgie (page 23), and the pine woods above (page 25), mark only half-way points in this longest of Scottish glens whose western outlet is Rannoch Moor – but no road leads all the way through.

Returning to Fortingal, and stopping at the churchyard to marvel at the ancient ewe tree which at over 3,000 years is said to be the oldest piece of living vegetation in Europe, the road continues east to Aberfeldy where the Tay is spanned by the famous Wade Bridge (page 27).

General Wade can be called the father of road building in the Highlands, though not all roads ascribed to him are his. The actual roads he built are as follows: Fort William to Fort Augustus, 1725; Fort Augustus to Inverness via Foyers, 1726; Inverness to Dunkeld, 1727–29; Crieff to Dalnacardoch by the Sma Glen, 1730–31; Dalwhinnie to Fort Augustus via the Corrieyairack, 1732; Catcleugh to Ruthven, 1733.

It has been said with truth in the Highlands that the roads are not much older than the railways, for it was not until 1801 that Thomas Telford began laying down the foundation of our modern road system and bridging the Tay at Dunkeld. The first stage coach in history ran the 117 miles from Inverness to Perth in 1809. The first train from Inverness crossed the Grampians by Drumochter and the Pass of Killiecrankie in 1863. The backward highlands were suddenly catching up.

Today Killiecrankie (page 29) is at the hub of modern tourism, with nearby Pitlochry, its shops, cinema, theatre, nature trails and hydro-electric station a constant attraction. Untold thousands drive along the Tummel Valley to admire the Queen's View and enjoy the fine range of forest walks. But west of Loch Rannoch the woods come to an end and so does the road. The great Moor of Rannoch lies between you and the peaks of Glen Coe, ten miles if you walk, but a long drive round back to the source of the Tay by car.

Like the approach to Loch Lomond where no hint is given of the geographical change ahead until you round a corner and suddenly the

Highlands are there, so it is with Glen Coe. You climb across the bleak Tibetan plateau of Rannoch Moor, then suddenly before you is the rock wedge of Buchaille Etive Mor as portal, but even this dramatic mountain does not prepare you for the narrowing trench and the thrust of its overpowering crags. In winter it is savagely alpine (page 31), a vertical world of black and white. In summer (page 33) when the grass is rich green and the crags grey-pink you feel the charm of the place where a massacre shocked the clans, not so much for the killing, but for the inhuman manner of it.

It is said that the reason why Campbell of Glen Lyon and his clan were chosen to carry out the massacre was because of an old sore against the Macdonalds who had cleaned their glen of cattle while the menfolk were away, thereby causing great hardship to the Campbells.

But cattle reiving was a sport as well as a necessity in the wilder glens where there was never enough sustenance to go round. Also, the normal condition in the Highlands was internecine warfare, and the power of the chief was measured by the number of fighting men he could raise. The Highlands had neither been governed by the Scottish or the English kings until after the brutal repressions following the '45.

The 1715 Rising was plotted on the opposite side of the Highlands in a glen that penetrates the Cairngorms (page 35). You can see the 'Punch Bowl' at the Linn of Quoich where the Earl of Mar stirred a huge mixture of punch into a natural pot-hole of the river as they discussed the plans which were to perish at Sheriffmuir. The clansfolk of Upper Deeside were still loyal Jacobites in 1745, and when the Rising was over many were cleared from the remoter glens because they were thought to be a menace to peace.

The interesting contrast of the eastern Highlands, the high Grampians, is the way they swell up from the Lowland plain of Strathmore and the Howe of the Mearns (page 37), where attractive villages like Fettercairn are backed by heathery hills but overlook superlative corn and cattle lands stretching right down to the North Sea.

Cross the first wave of these heathery billows and you are into Royal Deeside. August is the time when the purple moors are at their best, giving out heady scents and making rich contrast with the yellow barley as you cross the marginal farmlands for the heights (page 39).

It is enlightening to drive across the hills from the Dee to the Spey. Do this and you see the similarities of these two great river valleys which are separated from each other by the granite mass of the Cairngorms whose 4,000-foot plateau is a true fragment of the arctic in Britain. The late lying snows feed both rivers rendering them almost impervious to drought, and their springs produce the finest whisky in the world.

The River Dee bubbles out of the stones of Braeriach as a spring and after 85 miles swills into the North Sea at Aberdeen. The Spey rises much further to the west, at tiny Loch Spey, 1,142 feet above sea level, and needs 100 miles to reach Spey Bay near Elgin. Loch Spey lies close to the Corrieyairack, where General Wade built his military road over the 2,543-foot pass to effect quick movement between Ruthven Barracks on the Spey and Fort Augustus on Loch Ness in the Great Glen.

The Great Glen is the other mighty geological division of the Highlands. But in this case it slices through the peaks from the Atlantic to the North Sea. The glen forms a low pass under Ben Nevis and the Grey Corries range (page 41) whose rivers and lochs form a natural waterway which became the Caledonian Canal (page 43). Cromwell in 1651 was using a transport ship on Loch Ness to subdue the Highlanders, and General Wade was trying to achieve the same result when he built the Fort Augustus garrison in 1715. Some of the latter buildings are now incorporated in the present Benedictine abbey.

West of the Fort William entrance to the Caledonian Canal runs the scenic road to Mallaig, and above it for the most part runs the railway. Only by train can one get a full appreciation of Loch Shiel (page 45) and the monument at its head where a lonely figure looks inland to the Rough Bounds of Knoydart. It was from here the clans marched away to cross the Corrieyairack in the last Jacobite Rising of 1745. The sea lies just a short distance ahead, the open Atlantic with the splintered peaks of the Cuillins of Skye offset by the strange volcanic shapes of Eigg, Muck and Rhum which are known as the Small Isles.

Skye and the Small Isles, and the Outer Hebrides which lie still further west, were once part of the Highland plateau before the eroded land surface submerged and the loser valleys were drowned to become sea lochs. On the western mainland these are seen most spectacularly in the fjords stretching from Ardnamurch Point northwards to Cape Wrath. Loch Duich (page 47) is a good example, opening out as it does to Loch Alsh and a complex of Atlantic waterways between the Sound of Sleat and the Inner Sound where Applecross, Raasay and Skye face each other. Kyle of Lochalsh, the hub of the region, provides the quickest and cheapest crossing to Skye.

Skye is a little world of its own (page 49) with its crofting wings under the serrated peaks of the Cuillins and the weird pinnacles of the Quirang, where the Gaelic language still prevails and the smell of peat tangs the air. A good fast road runs from Kyle of Lochalsh to Uig, car ferry terminal for North Uist and Harris, but Skye is a place to tarry over, and its magical corners and crofting townships take time to explore. The best month is June, for freshness, clear air and sunshine.

Loch Carron, which faces Skye across the Inner Sound (page 51), is spanned by the Kyle railway line along its southern shore, with the steep rock terraces of the Applecross peaks rising to the north. The coast of Britain reaches its greatest depth between Applecross and Raasay, at over 1,000 feet, which is why these waters are coveted by oil platform builders and the Royal Navy who have a torpedo testing base here.

From the head of Loch Carron there is now a good road link into Glen Torridon, while Applecross itself has a coast road along Loch Torridon where until the 1970s there was only a footpath. Glen Torridon along its north side is jointly owned by the National Trust for Scotland and the Nature Conservancy. Both bodies have information centres and tourists are invited to walk the paths and enjoy the Nature Trails of some of the most spectacular mountain scenery in the Western Highlands.

North across Loch Maree rises the peak of Slioch, 3,217 feet, whose spade shape of summit is of warm sandstone overlaid on grey bumps of the older Lewisian gneiss. No roads penetrate this country north of Slioch, but a network of superb footpaths criss-cross it to Dundonnel on Little Loch Broom, and to Poolewe on Loch Ewe (page 53).

Driving from Loch Carron to Poolewe, or walking through the wild mountains you appreciate the truth that the boldest mountain scenery makes the poorest agriculture, for the ground is poverty-stricken for agriculture, except where there are raised beaches round the heads of lochs, or there is a depth of soil on headlands such as at Gairloch or Loch Ewe (page 55).

Of all the Torridonian peaks, none has more soaring beauty of form than An Teallach. Situated above Little Loch Broom and rising in a wall of rock terraces ending in a splintered crest, it presents one of the best summit ridges outside the Cuillins of Skye (page 57).

Northward again, beyond Ullapool, the strange sandstone peaks take on a weird and monolithic form, each standing alone and separated from its neighbour by lochans trapped in rough billows of grey gneiss. This is the country of Coigach and Assynt where rock accounts for more than half of the land surface. Suilven, 2,399 feet (page 59), is the most striking of all the peaks in the far north, a monument to the power of erosion.

Inchnadamph is the centre for exploring Assynt, where limestone outcrops at the head of Loch Assynt, and alpine flowers normally associated with the high corries, grow almost down to the hotel. Fishermen and mountaineers will find plenty to interest them here, while the caves of the Traligall Burn and the Allt nan Uamh still await exploration by pot-holers. Careful drivers, accustomed to the surprises of single-track winding roads in rocky country, should spend a day on the circuit from Inchnadamph to Lochinver and south down the exciting coast to return by Loch Lurgan and the A837.

To go on due north up the west coast means crossing the meeting of the lochs by free ferry at Kylesku, where the major fjord of Loch Cairnbawn splits into the two arms of lochs Glendhu and Glencoul. Tortuous driving on a single-width road lies on the far side, leading in ten exciting miles of bogs and rock to the joyful limestone greens of Scourie.

The Cambrian limestone which gives Scourie its farms and crofting fields was laid down only 500–600 million years ago, so it is a very recent formation compared to the gneiss and the Torridonian rocks which surround them. The same is true of the shining quartzite which gives the bald appearance to the peaks of the far north-west just round the corner east of Laxford Bridge.

These are the peaks of the Reay Forest, and the best impression of them is from Loch Stack (page 61), looking across to the near peak of Arkle. No hills in Scotland offers rougher walking than the Fionaven group of Reay. But the rewards are high for lovers of solitude, as you stride the tops with the Orkneys and the Outer Hebrides rising on the sea before you.

Motoring over the hump of the Reay from Rhiconich to Durness there is a point where you get a view up Strath Dionard to Fionaven 2,980 feet, the Cambrian quartzite country destitute of trees which was the last stronghold of the pine marten until the 1950s when it began to extend its range. Thanks to Forestry Commission woods, this nocturnal animal which can outrun a deer and outclimb a squirrel has reached down from the north as far south as Perthshire.

Few peat deserts in Scotland can appear so utterly hostile in slashing rain and dark clouds as the dreary hump of the Reay. So the feeling of welcome is all the greater as you drop from 500 feet to the yellow sands of the narrow Kyle of Durness, cross a turfy neck of limestone-rich land, and find yourself in a cheery village fringed by good farms above inlets of the Atlantic whose waters have the green clarity of an aquarium (page 63).

Durness has a population of 400 and a thriving craft village where craftsmen and women from many parts of Britain have settled in to make fine objects in exchange for a Highland way of life.

Ben Hope, the most northerly peak on the mainland of Scotland over 3,000 feet, lies just south-east above Strath More offering a fine route along narrow roads to Lairg. Or you may prefer to drive on to the Kyle of Tongue and to Bettyhill before turning down south by Strath Naver.

The far north has its own very special charm. But so has each district described in this book. Each visitor has his own preference. A lifetime is not long enough to explore any one in absolute detail, such is the lure of this land of sea and mountains.

The Plates

LOCH LOMOND

The 'Bonny Banks' are seen here from Duncryne Hill, Gartocharn, where the Lowlands meet the Highlands on the middle-distance islands forming the Highland Boundary Fault. The peaks are those of the Luss Hills, centre, and the Arrochar Hills, right.

Loch Lomond is 22·64 miles long. Its maximum depth, just north of Tarbet, is 623 feet, and at 27–45 square miles, its surface area is the greatest of any freshwater loch in Scotland. On its main islands, occupying the broad southern section of the loch, a holiday population builds up to about 200 in summer, but in winter it reduces to no more than 20 permanent inhabitants scattered between Inchfad, Inchmurrin and Inchtavannach.

One of the best ways of enjoying the most scenic parts of Loch Lomond is to make for Balmaha on the south-eastern shore and take the island mail boat which sails at 10·50 a.m., weather permitting, on Mondays, Thursdays and Saturdays in summer; Mondays and Thursdays in winter. From Balmaha a quick landing can be made on the nearby island of Inchcailloch which offers one of the most enchanting Nature Trail walks in Britain.

Anglers will find in Loch Lomond a bigger variety of fish than in any other Scottish loch, including the powan, the freshwater herring which is a left-over from the Ice Age.

On the western side the winding A82 runs the whole length of Loch Lomond. On the eastern side the narrow road comes to an end at Rowardennan beneath Ben Lomond in the Queen Elizabeth Forest Park. A passenger ferry from Rowardennan to Inverbeg connects west and east shores. Walkers and climbers will find a big variety of expeditions open to them.

THE TROSSACHS

The name 'Trossachs' means the 'Bristly Country' and applies to the scenic pass between Loch Katrine and Loch Achray. Sir Walter Scott and William Wordsworth came to it from Loch Lomond, by landing at Inversnaid, driving to Loch Katrine, and being rowed down to the end of the loch where the confusion of tree-clad rocks and bluffs burst upon them with delight.

Today the link between Loch Lomond and the Trossachs is even closer, because the Queen Elizabeth Forest Park embraces both. The view here is of Loch Achray in October when this small-scale prickly country is at its most colourful.

For sheer good forestry planning the Achray Forest between here and Aberfoyle is almost in a class of its own. To see it to best effect, take the zig-zagging road out of Aberfoyle climbing swiftly to nearly 800 feet. Leave your car at the lay-by for the panoramic viewpoint, and climb up to the stone indicator. See how the rocks and ridges are penetrated by oak and birch and the blue sheen of Sitka spruce.

Nature has acted as forester as well as man, by blowing down blocks of timber, and the replanting has resulted in trees of different sizes and greater variety than man the forester had planned. The fact that larches take a better grip of the soil than spruces has been used to good effect, for now we get their rich colours of green in spring and yellow in autumn on rocky ridge crests where it can be seen to greatest effect.

Altogether there is something like 170 miles of forest tracks in the Queen Elizabeth Forest Park, 40 of them waymarked and much used by pony trekkers and ramblers. In terms of timber productivity the output of the forest was 20,000 tons in 1974, and it should rise to 70,000 by 1992. The forestry labour force within the park is 65.

BEN LUI

The month is February, the spade-shaped mountain just left of centre is Ben Lui, and the foreground Highlanders, hardiest of all cattle, are munching a more than welcome ration of hay put out for them on the hard-frozen snow. Highland cattle are slow developers, they put on weight very gradually, but what they build up is stamina and great hardihood in a climate that can produce a heat wave in April or a blizzard in June.

The mountain, Ben Lui (3,708 feet) is a notable one on three main counts. To mountaineers, the steep shadowy corrie facing north-east provides superb winter climbs of alpine character. To botanists the same corrie in summer is one of the most noted in Scotland for alpine plants. To geographers the corrie is even more significant, because in it rises the infant Tay, curling eastwards through Strath Fillan and Glen Dochart to enter Loch Tay at Killin.

To reach the corrie of Ben Lui, take the track to Coninish Farm, and follow up the silver thread of stream emerging from the bowl whose upper part is usually snowfilled until well into June. Walkers intent on the summit should take the easy left or right slopes, avoiding the corrie. Alpinists looking for the steepest routes do not need any advice, but straight up the centre of the gully is as good a route as any.

Botanists will find amongst the mica-schist rocks and broken screes everything that makes this mountain so exciting. Nor is it necessary to go into the more difficult part of the steeper corrie. The most rewarding time is the first week in July when the mountain is in full flower following the retreat of the winter snow.

GLEN LYON

Glen Lyon has been called the glen of the three L's, the longest, the loneliest, and the loveliest. The scene here is at Bridge of Balgie, midway up the motorable part of the glen, between Fortingal and Loch Lyon. No single place in Scotland has more charm than this particular spot where the Lyon roars below the old bridge and foams into a dark pool where salmon lie.

The joy of Glen Lyon is not only its trees, but its variety. At Fortingal where the strath is broad it would be easy to pass on, not realising that a narrow glen penetrates the steep hills. Turn west and you are in a defile, with the River Lyon tumbling through the ravine far below and rock walls hemming you on the other side. It is an exciting place at any time, but in autumn it can be thrilling beyond words, when the gorge is a veritable rainbow of colour.

The wealth of broad-leaved trees continues, sycamores, beeches, oaks, rowans, ash, chestnuts, giving way to birches growing high amongst the grey screes of the mountain flanks. Beyond the Pass of Lyon, farmers have to cope with peaks rising nearly 4,000 feet on the south side, and 3,400 feet on the north. Yet they get their crops in most years, knowing as they do how to make the most of every good hour.

Glen Lyon was once a populous place, when the power of the clan chief was not in personal riches but in the number of fighting men he could muster. Even 100 years ago the glen had a population of 700. Today it is down to less than a sixth of that, though there is evidence that more and more people want to come and settle, if only in retirement. Alas, there is no source of income other than estate work, or catering for tourists, in this part of the world.

GLEN LYON, THE UPPER GLEN

The Lyon, beneath the Allt Conait, about four miles west of Bridge of Balgie, flows through a remnant of the ancient Caledonian forest of Scotland, where this photograph was taken. The pink-barked pines with umbrella canopies of bottle-green needles are growing near their limit and provide shelter for the wild red deer.

The red stag in the foreground was taken in October, in the rutting season, when the animals which have been running in the herd become solitary, and try to take possession of as many hinds as they can muster. At this time the glen echoes with deep-throated bellowings of challenging stags, as they face up to each other, fight, or give chase.

Glen Lyon is deer forest, and stalkers are out on the hills shooting stags until 20 October, when the stags are left in peace to get on with the rut. But the season for shooting hinds opens now, and continues until the end of February, when the deer population should be reduced to the number which the forest can support. If an annual cull of one-sixth of the herd is taken, deer numbers can remain constant. If no shooting is done, the deer become competitors with each other for the available food supply, with a decline in the quality of the animals. Also, the too numerous animals tend to become raiders of the farmers crops.

No other animal can use high ground so efficiently as red deer, and their survival through the centuries of over-burning and over-grazing of hills and forest is proof of their adaptability.

ABERFELDY – THE WADE BRIDGE

This graceful bridge of five arches spanning the Tay at Aberfeldy belongs to the very beginning of road building in the Highlands, yet it is still sound enough to carry an ever-increasing amount of modern traffic over its steep hump. It is worth parking off the main road at the golf course, and taking a walk over the bridge of grey chlorite schist to look at the 60 feet of its main arch, and read the inscription cut into the stone. It reads:

AT THE COMMAND OF
HIS MAJTY KING GEORGE 2 ND
THIS BRIDGE WAS ERECTED
IN THE YEAR 1733
THIS WITH THE ROADS AND OTHER
MILITARY WORKS FOR SECURING
A SAFE AND EASY COMMUNICATION
BETWEEN THE HIGH LANDS AND
THE TRADING TOWNS IN THE LOW

COUNTRY WAS BY HIS MAJTY
COMMITTED TO THE CARE OF LIEUT
GENERAL GEORGE WADE
COMMANDER IN CHIEF OF THE FORCES
IN SCOTLAND WHO LAID THE FIRST
STONE OF THIS BRIDGE ON THE
23RD OF APRIL AND FINISHED THE
WORK IN THE SAME YEAR.

Between 1723 and 1740 General Wade built a network of nearly 250 miles of military roads, using ordinary soldiers as labourers in building seasons lasting from May to October. Until Wade built this bridge at Aberfeldy, the river was forded by ferry. The bridge was a key point in the military road from Dalnacardoch, crossing by way of Tummel Bridge to Aberfeldy and on to Crieff.

The route Wade had opened up was to prove invaluable to cattle drovers heading for the great markets of Crieff and Falkirk. By the latter part of the eighteenth century other new bridges had been built over some of the larger rivers, but not until Thomas Telford began his great road building programme in 1803 was there a serious effort to tackle the problem of communications for the economic betterment of the Highlanders.

26

THE PASS OF KILLIECRANKIE

North of Pitlochry the Inverness train climbs through the autumn-brilliant Pass of Killiecrankie on a ledge of stone high above the gorge of the River Garry, one of the most impressive passages of the Highland Line. The stone viaduct of 10 arches is 508 feet long. From the parapet to the foundations is a plunge of 54 feet, and the train is just about to enter a 128-yard tunnel. The building of this line from Inverness across the Grampians is one of the great stories of railway engineering.

The man who conceived it was Joseph Mitchell, Chief Inspector of Roads and Bridges under Thomas Telford. Mitchell was planning to build a line across the Grampians as early as 1845, yet the railway did not reach Perth until 1848. But Mitchell was too far ahead of his time. He had to wait until 1861 before Government approval was given to his wild plan. And once begun he built the 104 miles of line between Dunkeld and Forres in 23 months.

The hold-up in getting started was due to the rival Great North of Scotland Railway Coy. who favoured a coastal route from Inverness via Aberdeen. They won the Parliamentary battle, but failed to take their option. Mitchell's route had shortened the journey from Inverness to the south by 60 miles, and his methods of building were so economic that he reduced the normal costs of railroad construction by about a third.

Thanks to North Sea Oil and the industrial revolution in the Moray Firth region the line is being upgraded for increased use.

GLEN COE

In the narrow Pass of Glen Coe, nature has contrived a geographical masterpiece. The view here is from a point where the road runs through rocky jaws, and looks across to the 'Lost Valley' running obliquely towards the sharp peak of Stob Coire nan Lochan (3,657 feet). The road passes under the projecting spurs on the right known as the 'Three Sisters'. The photograph was taken in February, and shows the bitter conditions of the month in which the infamous 'Massacre' took place.

This 'Lost Valley' is where the Macdonalds of Glen Coe used to hide their stolen cattle. It was on 13 February 1692 Campbell of Glen Lyon carried out an act of treachery unparalleled in Highland history to that time. He accepted hospitality over a period lasting from 1 February, assuring the Macdonalds that Argyll's regiment came only in peace.

But Campbell was given his final orders as he played cards with his MacIain his host. They were: '. . . to fall upon the rebells the Macdonalds of Glencoe and put all to the sword under 70. You are to take special care that the old fox and his sons do not escape your hand. You are to secure all avenues that no man escape. This you are to put into execution at five of the clock precisely. . . .'

The murders began in the darkness. MacIain was shot in the back. The soldiers used their teeth to get the rings off his wife's fingers, stripping her of her clothes. Women, children, boys were amongst the slain. The houses were put to fire. But Campbell could show only 38 bodies. The others had escaped, some to slow death in the snowy hills. Yet the bad weather was a friend as well as a foe, for blizzards delayed another force of troops intent on cutting off their escape.

The blame for the Massacre must lie with King William who caused the Campbell's to carry out the act of extirpation after they had taken the oath of allegiance. The oath should have been taken on 1 February. It was taken on the 6th. The Massacre of the 13th did not even have an excuse.

30

GLEN COE

The view here is on descent from the summit of the Pass where the narrow glen opens out to Loch Triochatan and the rock pyramid of Stob Coire nam Beith comes into view behind the nose of Ant-Sron on its right. The white cottage of Achnambeithach is only 240 feet above sea level. A steep path follows the right hand side of the stream and threads its way into the corrie cirque, with at the head of it Bidian nam Bian (3,766 feet), highest summit in Glen Coe.

There is no summit in this cirque that can be regarded as being difficult for hill-walkers in summer. It is the complications of topography, allied to mist and changing conditions which makes them serious propositions. Mistakes are easily rectified on grassy hills. In Glen Coe where there is so much exposed rock plunging into narrow ravines, the climber must know where he is at all times, so careful work with the map and compass becomes a necessity.

For the rock climber Glen Coe offers some of the most elegant routes in Britain, and in severe winters when the gullies, ridges and faces become plastered with ice the mountains rank with the hardest in Scotland.

The contrast between this low end of the glen, where the mountains give way to the broadening strath is most striking. It was in this fertile strip that the Macdonalds lived with their herds of cattle. To escape on that fateful February morning of 1692 they had to break over the icy mountains into Glen Creran or Glen Etive. That so many survived is proof of their hardihood. The stricken Macdonalds were allowed to return and set up home again. And many of that name live around Glencoe village today.

DEESIDE

This is the country which was loved by Queen Victoria, and she called the stretching pines in the foreground 'the Bonniest Plaid in Scotland'. The scene is Ballochbuie in the Balmoral Estate, and through the stones in the foreground prattles the Garbh Allt, the rough burn. Far beyond can be seen the summer snows of Ben Avon, the most easterly of the high Cairngorms (3,843 feet).

Queen Victoria entered into possession of Ballochbuie on 15 May 1878, and she did Scotland a great service by saving this priceless fragment of primeval forest from the woodman's axe, for it was about to be felled. Now it is being valued and conserved, not only here, but on the other side of the Cairngorms where Rothiemurchus is a part-echo of Ballochbuie with the same exciting wild life.

These ancient woods do not form a close canopy like a commercial plantation. Widely spaced, and often with a fair amount of juniper growing amongst them, they are places where you expect things to happen; a capercaillie swerving through the trees like a turkey; crossbills flighting amongst the pines, siskins and redpolls constantly moving, the sight of a roe deer, and amongst the upper trees red deer stags and hinds. Eagles build their eyries in the pines, and hen harriers hunt the moors. On the high tops dotterel and snow buntings nest with ptarmigan in the only fragment of the high arctic in Britain where the great 4,000-foot plateau stretches from the Spey to the Dee without human habitation.

FETTERCAIRN

The charming village of Fettercairn lies under the Grampians, though the old name for this swelling range of hills separating the big fields of the Howe of the Mearns from the valley of the Dee is the 'Mounth'. Fettercairn has a grace of architecture suited to its situation between the Lowlands and the Highlands. Everything about it is attractive, the square, with the old market cross in its centre and the ornamental archway over the southern entrance of the town, and, beyond it, the inn where Queen Victoria and Prince Albert slept in 1861.

There are only three ways to break from the Lowlands directly across the Grampians by car: from Blairgowrie by the Devil's Elbow; from Stonehaven by the Slug road to Banchory; or most scenic of all, from Fettercairn by the Cairn o' Mounth which climbs swiftly to 1,488 feet.

From up there in the heather you look across one of the great divisions of Scotland, with the agricultural quilt of the Lowlands spread out in all its glory of fields and farms stretching to the Tay and Forth, while west and north stretches leagues of hill and heather cut by such glens as Esk, Lethnot, Clova, Prosen and Isla which have no through-roads.

Immediately south-west of Fettercairn, near Edzell, the hill fort known as the White Caterthun should be visited. Here, on a hill top, behind a 470-foot enclosure, 220 feet wide, lived the farmers of 2,000 years ago in their fortress villages.

These Celtic farmers of the Iron Age were the first permanent settlers. Earlier people had been forced to keep on the move as they exhausted the resources of the land. But the agriculture of the Celts was based on the plough. They were cultivators and stock breeders. But they needed to feel safe from attack, so they built hilltop forts to house their families and to retire to at night. In Fettercairn you are in the heart of Pictland.

BETWEEN THE DEE AND THE SPEY

The scene here is west of Tarland, looking over the ripe barley to the purple heather where the by-roads climb over uplands to the Lecht, traversing some of the finest and most expensive grouse moors in Scotland. You have to concentrate on the intricacies of the high climbing road to Cockbridge, twisting up to 2,000 feet as it does in the snowiest country in Scotland. Not surprisingly this is usually the first road to be blocked every winter, and the last to be cleared.

Even in summer it is exciting, as you leave the bleak heights and plunge down into Strathavon where human life resumes once more, with noble undulations of farms and fields, with woods planted in the form of shelter belts. Here you see how the big fields have been won from the moors, how the birches cluster where they can find a foothold, and how men can make a blanket of spruces replace heather when they have a mind to.

This is one of the best and biggest pieces of landscaping in the Highlands, and even if the landowners say the forestry side of it is uneconomic because of the smallness of the units, it is first-class ecology.

Beyond Tomintoul (1,160 feet), highest village in the Highlands, you climb again, diving into Glen Brown, then up to 1,400 feet for the swing down into Strathspey and a view of the steep northern rampart of the Cairngorms. The great river valleys of the Spey and the Dee have a basic similarity, in the roll of the gentle hills backing the broad straths, and in the pattern of woods and farmlands on soils left behind as the glaciers of the past slowly melted. The notably bracing air makes these valleys ideal for sporting holidays.

LOCHABER

This is the district known as Lochaber, and the peaks are those of the Grey Corries rising in a line of snowy summits due south of Spean Bridge. The photograph, taken with a foreground of birch and pine, was taken in April from a point just north of Gairlochy in Cameron of Lochiel's country.

So between the foreground of the trees and the snows of the mountains lies the trench of the Great Glen, the dramatic fracture where the Northern Highlands slipped away from the Grampians. Erosion along the fault line created the basins occupied by the chain of lochs which Thomas Telford was to link by building the Caledonian Canal from the Atlantic entrance beneath Ben Nevis to Inverness on the Moray Firth.

The total distance of the Canal is 60 miles, but the extraordinary thing for such a mountain country is that the summit is a mere 115 feet, with nature providing natural lochs for a third of the distance. The work began at the top and bottom end of the canal in 1803 and Watt thought his 20-foot canal could be built in seven years. It took 19 years to open the passage, by which time James Watt's steam engine was replacing sails as a mode of propulsion and the canal was too small for the ships being built.

However the canal is still in use. Its locks are fully mechanised and an increasing number of pleasure craft and fishing boats use it. No tourist ship operates its full length, but there is a daily sailing from Inverness in the converted ice-breaker Scot II. It is also possible to rent fibre-glass cabin cruisers and have a do-it-yourself holiday enjoying the kind of scenery shown in this photograph.

LOCH NESS

This October photograph shows a characteristic piece of the most famous of the Caledonian Canal lochs. Loch Ness for most of its $22\frac{3}{4}$ miles is narrow, only two miles across at Urquart Bay where it is broadest. But it is so uniformly deep and shaped like a bathtub that it holds $2\frac{1}{2}$ times more water than Loch Lomond, with a maximum depth of 754 feet. Only Loch Morar is deeper at 1,077 feet, and it too is said to have a monster. Morag has put the fear of death into anglers attacked by it in a boat. Nessie has been hunted by men of all nationalities, but so far nothing very conclusive has turned up, though scientists have come back with evidence of 'something'.

The monster has a respectable origin. In literature it appears about AD565 in *The Life of St. Columba* by St. Adamnan, Abbot of Iona. St. Columba is described as driving it back with prayer in the River Ness as its open mouth was about to take a swimming man. However, it made no more appearance in history until 1932, since when you could produce a queue of respected people who claim to have seen it, including a monk at Fort Augustus Benedictine Monastery.

There are various descriptions varying from sightings of '. . . a huge snail with a long neck' to that of an animal with several humps and a head like a horse. A case has been made that it is a huge worm, able to make humps and narrow its neck. There is a wide literature and you can take your pick of possibilities, ranging from sea serpents to relatives of Tullimonstrum gregarium, a fossil creature of 280 million years ago and discovered in America in 1958.

Monster or not, the loch is more interesting for having the possibility of a sighting. And even if you should see nothing, the looking and hoping does add a spice of interest to the long drive up Loch Ness.

LOCH SHIEL

Few places in the Western Highlands are more steeped in history than the head of Loch Shiel where a Prince, carved in stone, looks inland to the Knoydart hills from the top of a tall column. The monument commemorates the Highlanders who fought and died for Bonny Prince Charlie, who raised the clans here on 21 August 1745. The monument was built by Alexander MacDonald of Glenaladale in 1815, but the figure of the Prince which crowns it was not added until 1831.

Loch Shiel is a freshwater loch cutting seawards through uninhabited country. The track on the left is private and maintained by the Forestry Commission. It goes to Polloch where there is a Forestry Village. The public way of getting to this remote settlement is from Strontian in Ardnamurchan over a difficult hill pass.

The very remoteness of this country favoured the Prince when he was on the run after Culloden. Look to the hills behind the big curving railway viaduct and before you is the setting of one of the greatest man-hunts in history. The Prince escaped thanks to the courage and devotion of his Highland companions who broke the cordon.

Just 15 miles or so west of the head of Loch Shiel close to the Mallaig road you will find another little monument, 'the cairn of the departure'. The inscription reads:

This by tradition is the rock from which the Prince left Scotland on 20th September 1746, leaving behind him immortal glory and immortal sorrow; and heroes who fought, not counting the odds, for troth and kingship and clanship love; and shieling and song and the ways of the Gael.

LOCH DUICH

The smooth surfaced double-width road along the north shore of Loch Duich is something not to be taken for granted, for just round the corner is Kyle of Lochalsh, where single-track road with passing places is resumed.

The Loch Duich road was completed only in 1972 after more than a decade of dirty work in all weathers. The traveller driving over from Invergarry on the Great Glen should pay attention to it, for the road is threading a very wild country of high jostling peaks. First you have the climb from Loch Garry to a point where you can look into the Rough Bounds of Knoydart where Bonny Prince Charlie and his men broke the enemy cordon.

Then you plunge into Glen Moriston and along the side of bleak Loch Cluanie to enter the narrows of Glen Shiel winding between thrusting ridges to hit the head of Loch Duich and wind along its enchanting shore to Dornie village where the fjord splits. The widening arm ahead is called Lochalsh and Skye is just across the water. The narrow fjord going off north-eastward is Loch Long.

This photograph looks along Loch Duich on a May morning when the yellow gorse was fragrant and primroses and violets starred the banks. But the snow patches on the sharp peak of Scuir Ouran (3,305 feet) show it is still wintry up there, with the hills showing no sign of growth. Yet up there at 2,000 feet the first of the arctic alpines was blooming, purple saxifrage and moss campion.

Even the motorist cocooned in his car notices the difference in climate between the heights of Glen Shiel and the mild seaside air of the sea lochs, which has a magical quality of fresh softness.

SKYE

This is the crofting township of Tarskavaig in the south-west corner of the 'Winged Isle', and the peak rising behind it is Blaven.

Times change and so does crofting. Once upon a time, less than 50 years ago, there was competition for crofts, on good land especially where there was sea fishing, as here, to assure subsistence in bad agricultural times. But there was never enough land to go round, and down the centuries young and able men had to leave home, seeking their fortune as soldiers or emigrating to better themselves.

Nowadays the croft, however good, is not regarded as a viable proposition, unless there is a job and wages behind it, or retirement pensions. To pay for electricity, the washing machine, the television set, the motor car, the Highlander and islander needs money, like everyone else. And if he cannot get it, he leaves, keeping his croft as a holiday home, or selling it perhaps at an inflated price.

The tourist industry, particularly in Skye, has been valuable in keeping crofts going, especially nowadays when the season begins as early as March and lasts until the end of October.

Gone are the primitive dwellings which shocked travellers to the Highlands and islands 50 years ago. With earth floors, smoky interiors and little in the way of sanitation, the thatched roofs on rough stones were more akin to Neolithic dwellings than twentieth-century homes.

These old houses have been mostly swept away, or are now used as byres for cattle. Crofting, at its lowest level, is an uneconomic use of manpower, because almost its whole work centres around providing winter keep for a cow or two and a few sheep, without providing a real living or worthwhile surplus of stock. Yet on a higher level where the land is good it has been valuable in keeping communities like Tarskavaig together, because crofting is a communal way of life, with many tasks shared, peat cutting, clipping and dipping of sheep, the handling of boats, and even the building of houses like the ones shown.

48

PLOCKTON

Whatever future stir the building of oil platforms may bring to the Loch Carron area, it is safe to say that the little village of Plockton will remain aloof from it, thanks to the promontory on which it sits, sheltering it from the west winds and giving it an outlook across a delightful bay to the bold rock bluffs thrusting grey rock buttresses above the turrets of Duncraig Castle.

Built as a well-planned fishing village at the end of the eighteenth century, Plockton became an important centre for schooners trading with the Baltic. Alas however, with the failure of inshore fishing in the mid-nineteenth century, Plockton declined like the other fishing villages of this west coast.

The building of the Kyle Line and work on the railway was important to its survival, but crofting, like Plockton Gaelic, has largely died out. Of nine registered crofters, only one makes a whole-time living and one a part-time living out of the land. Of all the houses, about half are occupied only in summer, as holiday homes. In view of the current shortage of houses for workers, it is a pity the Highland Development Board did not buy up every house as it came on the market for sale, so that people wishing to live and work in the Western Highlands could have homes at reasonable rent.

However Plockton still contains a lively local population who enjoy sailing and run their own regattas. The village has its own air-strip, and in summer a large camp and caravan site on the Plock swells the population considerably.

Yachtsmen have the best of it here, since Loch Carron opens out on the Inner Sound, with Applecross, Raasay and Skye just across the water, while round the corner is Lochalsh and the Sound of Sleat. A magical place on a magical coast of lochs and remote mountains.

LOCH EWE AND POOLEWE

Poolewe village lies round the head of Loch Ewe and is backed by the greatest wilderness area remaining in Scotland. The mountains, left, are those of the Fisherfield Forest, spanned only by pony tracks. Ancient Lewisian gneiss rises to the summits of some of these peaks, as on Beinn Arry Charr seen on the left. In this great area between the north shore of Loch Maree and Little Loch Broom nobody lives permanently. The country is too bleak and sterile, which makes the contrasts of Poolewe all the greater, for growing here at sea level are some of the most exotic plants in Britain.

The famous Inverewe Gardens, now in the care of the National Trust for Scotland, are on the promontory on the left of the picture, and were the inspiration of Osgood Mackenzie, son of the twelfth chief of Gairloch. Mackenzie, who died in 1922, planted the pine trees, and waited 20 years for them to grow up, before he began to build his garden in their shelter.

Poolewe has the same geographical latitude as parts of Siberia, but thanks to the Gulf Stream, and the shelter which Mackenzie provided he was able to boast before his death that any plant which will grow in the open at Kew will grow here. Visitors come to Inverewe from all over the world nowadays, and it can be said with certainty that whether they come from the hotter spots of the equator or the alpine heights of the Himalayas, they will find plants they know at home growing in the open here on what was once a stark and stony headland of the Western Highlands.

Poolewe has a fine camping and caravan site run in conjunction with the National Trust for Scotland. One of its innovations is a covered space for wet-weather tenting. There is also a laundry, drying room and showers.

52

TUIRNAIG

Two miles north of Poolewe the coast road climbs over the hill to Gruinard Bay, and the visitor intent on enjoying a superb panorama should visit the National Trust for Scotland viewpoint sited at Tuirnaig. This is the southerly part of that panorama, looking to the jostling summits of the Torridonian hills lying southward of Loch Maree. These mountains, which are shared jointly between the Nature Conservancy and the National Trust for Scotland, offer some of the best walking and climbing in the Highlands in a region notable for natural pine forest and striking rock form.

The traveller in these parts soon discovers that the more striking the scenery, the poorer the agriculture. Crofting exists here only on the coastal strips, and even so, something like 50 per cent of the crofts in this part of the world are no longer worked. Tourism and work on the naval base are the mainstays of local employment in the Poolewe and Aultbea area; and Gairloch just south of Poolewe is a fish-landing port.

This was a very poorly served region by road until the potato famine of 1846–48, when the destitute crofters had to be found work, and Osgood Mackenzie's mother came to the rescue, paying them a wage to drive the road up the western shore of Loch Maree, doling out oatmeal to supplement the shellfish boiled in milk which was all the coastal crofters could find to eat.

The former remoteness of these parts has vanished. Over 100,000 visitors come to Inverewe Gardens every year now, and at peak times hotels and bed-and-breakfast houses can hardly cope with the demand. Single-width driving still congests the roads in Glen Torridon and Applecross. But the true delight of the Highlands is not to travel great distances trying to see as much as possible, but to settle down and get to know one part intimately, preferably on your own two feet.

AN TEALLACH

The road from Poolewe to Ullapool takes you past this splendid ridge of pink sandstone and white quartzite collectively known as An Teallach – The Forge. It was taken from the roadside larches near Dundonnel on a May morning after a night of keen frost, when all the vivid colour contrasts were at their best.

Only Liathach of Glen Torridon can rival An Teallach for architectural form. Both example the same perpendicularity of rock terracing which lift the peaks literally '. . . from riverbed to the sky'. Sir Archibald Geikie, one-time director of the Geological Survey in Scotland described them thus:

> At every turn their odd combination of steep rocky declivity and lines of horizontal terrace suggest gigantic exaggerations of human architecture. Screes of debris like stone-laden glaciers creep down into the corries below . . .

The finest walking excursion from Little Loch Broom for those interested in inaccessible places is to follow up the Garbh Allt stream from Dundonnel, and in four miles enter the rocky fastness of Loch Toll an Lochan, height 1,700 feet.

There is no special difficulty though the walking is rough. The best bit is where the stream foams white over pink rock slabs littered with erratic blocks and you climb up the edge of one of these stone-laden trails of debris. Then suddenly you come over the lip and you look on a tiny oval of loch hemmed by a cirque of savage pinnacles rising over 1,000 feet vertically from the corrie floor.

Another fine walk is to take the Allt Gleann Chaorachain pathway which crosses the shoulder of An Teallach in six miles, reaching the remote Strath na Sheallag where herds of stags and hinds feed by the river banks in May.

SUILVEN

North of Ullapool a fast double-width road carries you into the rocky country of Assynt whose dominant peak is Suilven in an area of sparse habitation and innumerable lochs. Because of the quantity of exposed rock surface, no other region of Highland country is so sensitive to changes of light. Suilven can change from deep blue, through purple to grey while you watch. It is an example of a Torridonian mountain in an extreme state of denudation, a sandstone peak on a plinth of Lewisian gneiss.

Travelling in Coigach and Assynt, where each peak stands alone it is hard to take in the fact the spaces between them were once filled up with the same sandstone, that they were once part of a vast plateau gradually broken down by the combined forces of erosion and glaciation until all that remains are fragments of its foundations.

A fine way to climb Suilven is from Inverkirkaig just south of Lochinver. The way is by the Fionn Loch, reached by five miles of easy walking on a made path. An easy gully leads to the hollow between the peaks; thereafter you have the delight of the summit ridge and a striking view of the denuded landscape – and its continuation in the Outer Hebrides, once part of the same plateau.

Visitors travelling north from Ullapool should not miss the chance of calling in at Knockan Cliff Visitor Centre to learn something of the geology and wild life of Assynt through which they will be touring. A 'Motor Trail' pamphlet enables you to interpret the landscape as you drive along. But if the weather is reasonable, do not miss the chance of walking the geological nature trail, where the rock structure of the peaks is superbly exposed and explained.

REAY FOREST

The word 'forest' in so many bare regions of the Highlands does not refer to trees, but to deer forest, and in the whole of the Western Highlands there is no hill barer than Arkle (2,580 feet) seen here over the pastures of Achfary at the head of Loch More, which is part of the Westminster Estate, with some of the best salmon fishing and deer stalking in the north-west. Roads pass east of the Reay Forest, from Altnahara by Strath More, and west by Loch Stack and the rock desert of Rhiconich, but there is no way across the range except by bridle tracks.

Laxford Bridge, seven miles north-west from where this photograph was taken, is the turning off point for the limestone oasis of Scourie whose greenery is in such contrast to the acid gneiss and Torridonian sandstone. And it is from here the remarkable bird island of Handa can be reached, its spectacular cliffs and 'stack' whirring with guillemots, razorbills and puffins, while round the inlets fulmar petrels soar endlessly to a background noise of screaming kittiwakes. Great skuas and red-throated divers haunt the lochs of Handa, and no summer visit to this tiny island is ever a disappointment. Handa is most easily reached from the crofting township of Tarbert, north of Scourie.

For walkers the best way of exploring the Reay peaks is from Achfary, by following the track round the eastern side of Loch Stack past the deserted house called 'Lone', and taking the footpath forking left. This brings the ridge of Arkle within easy reach and a varied traverse can be made by coming off the north peak to another path that takes you back to Loch Stack Lodge. Three miles of road walking would then take you back to your car.

SANGO BAY

Even in the rain there is an illusion of sunshine at Sango Bay, on the north western tip of Scotland. Durness is the nearest village to Cape Wrath, and the photograph was taken from the sand curves just east of the village looking towards Balnakeil. The hump in the distance is called The Parbh, in the roadless peaty interior just south of Cape Wrath Lighthouse.

A great contrast of country lies between Sango Bay and the Cape, which the Vikings called Hvarf, the turning point. Home to them would lie along the Pentland Firth and north by the Orkneys and Shetlands to Norway. To them this Durness coast was the Southern land, hence the name we know today as Sutherland.

And in all Sutherland there is no greener place than Durness, because of its limestone which is the basis of good farming. The narrowness of the strip makes it all the more vivid, when behind it are the peaks of Reay and on its far side the sombre fjord of Loch Eriboll, round which the road to John o' Groats wriggles.

The chance to visit Cape Wrath should not be missed. In summer there is a ferry service across the Kyle of Durness, and a minibus on the other side to bear you over the rough road to the cliff edge where the lighthouse stands, facing out to an ocean that continues without break to the arctic ice and the North Pole.

Only lightkeepers live permanently on the Parbh. There is no crofting township nearer than Sheigra, southward of Sandwood Bay. Eastward is even wilder, with cliffs rising to nearly 600 feet against which the Atlantic breakers hurl, submerging tall rock stacks at their base in wild weather. The golden eagle nests on these cliffs, sharing them with layers of seabirds whose echoing sound rises and falls with the echoing boom of the seas advancing and retreating. It is a fitting note on which to end the book.